What Babies Wear

by Anne Witherington
and Bobbie Neate

Contents

Emma's family tree	2
What babies wear today	4
What toddlers wear today	6
When Mum and Dad were babies	8
When Mum and Dad were toddlers	10
When grandparents were babies	12
When grandparents were toddlers	14
Great grandparents as babies	16
Great grandparents as toddlers	18
What babies wore long ago	20
What toddlers wore long ago	22
Glossary	23
Index	24

Emma's family tree

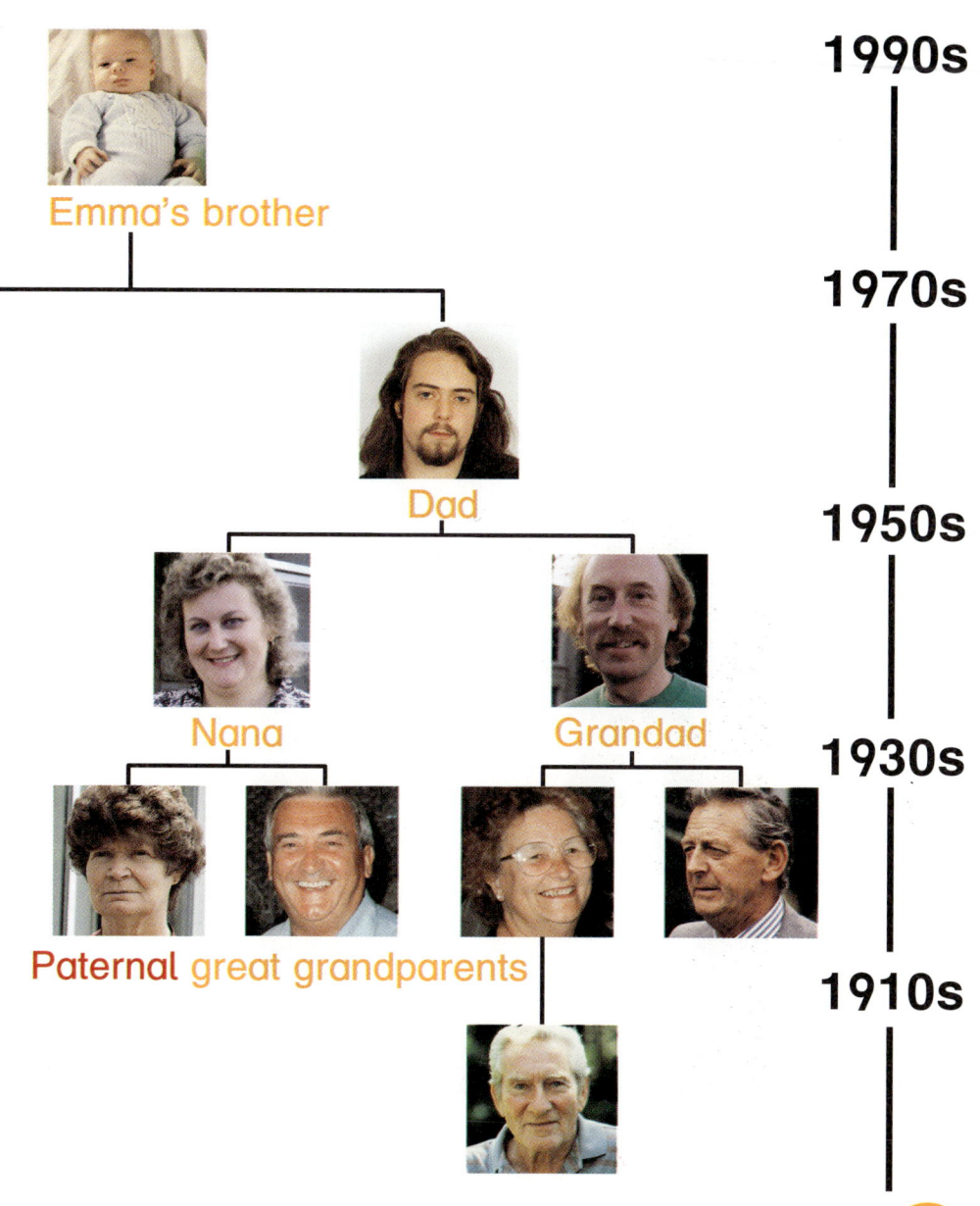

What babies wear today

Most babies wear nappies, vests and **bodysuits** when they are very small.

Emma's brother

Small babies are well wrapped up in cold weather.

1990s

Babies' vests are made from soft wool or cotton.
The bodysuit is made from stretchy material which lets the baby move its arms and legs freely.

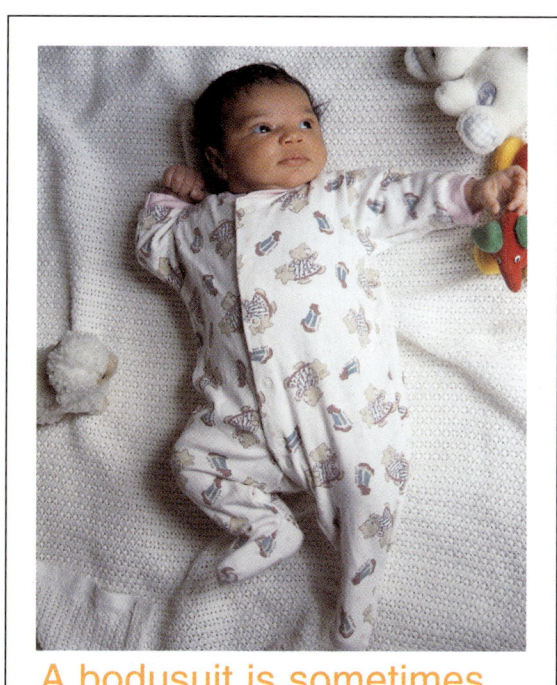

A bodysuit is sometimes called a Babygro.

What toddlers wear today

Nowadays toddlers can wear lots of different kinds of clothes. Parents choose clothes which are easy to wash.

Emma

Unisex clothes are worn by boys and girls.

1990s

Toddlers wear track suits and trousers.
They wear leggings and jumpers.
They wear shorts and tee shirts.
Girls sometimes wear skirts
or dresses.
Toddlers clothes are
often brightly coloured.

Shorts

Dungarees

Jacket

Hat

When Mum and Dad were babies

When mums and dads were small babies they sometimes

Mum Dad

wore bodysuits over their nappies. They wore **catsuits** and jumpers when they were a bit bigger.

Catsuits kept babies warm while they were playing on the floor.

1970s

Baby clothes were made from fabrics which were easy to wash.

Catsuits were usually made in dark colours so that they would not show dirt when the babies crawled around on the floor.

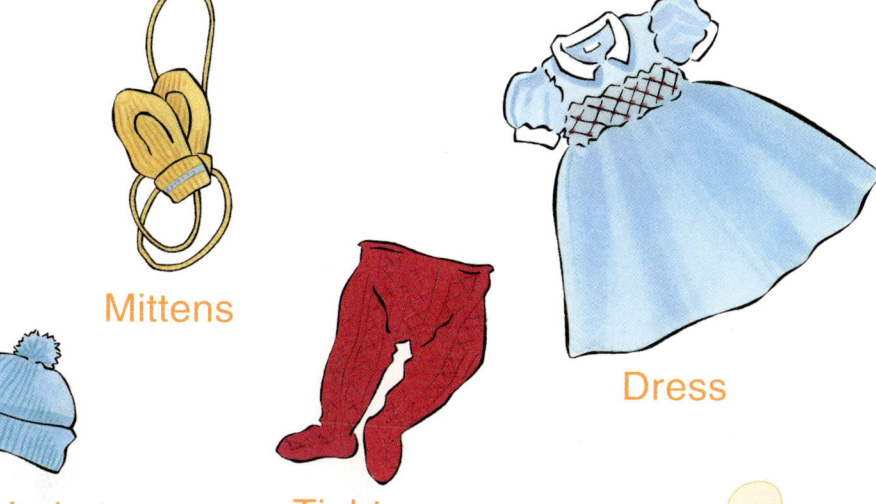

Mittens

Bobble hat

Tights

Dress

When Mum and Dad were toddlers

Many **fabrics** were used for toddlers clothes. **Nylon**, **crimplene** and **denim** were popular fabrics.

Mum

Dad

On special occasions your mum might have worn a frilly dress.

1970s

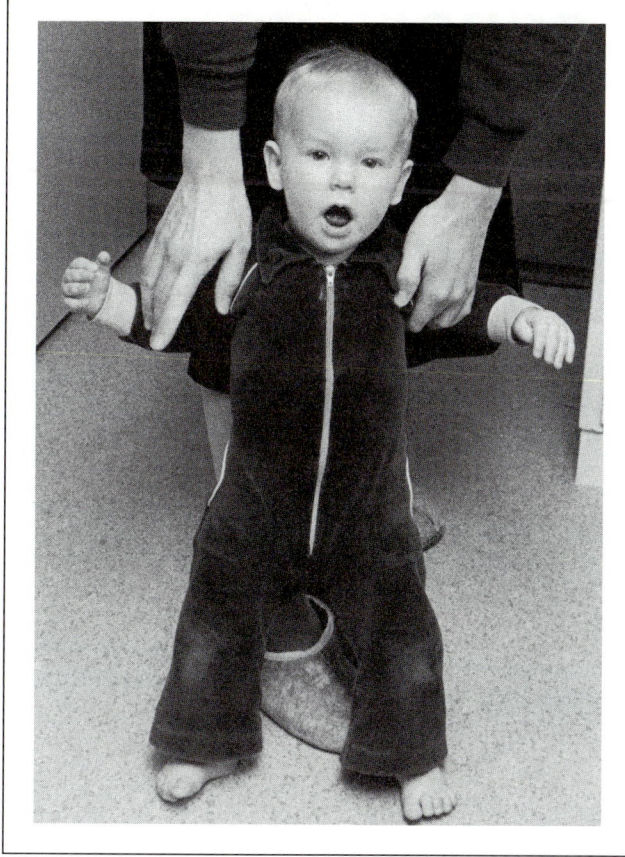

Your dad might have worn long trousers with **flared** bottoms.

Girls wore skirts or dresses with brightly coloured tights. Their shoes usually fastened across the front with a button.

Boys wore cotton or nylon shirts with long collars.

When grandparents were babies

Small babies wore nighties. The nighties were fastened at the back with long tapes. Most babies wore **terry towelling** nappies.

Grandma

Grandad

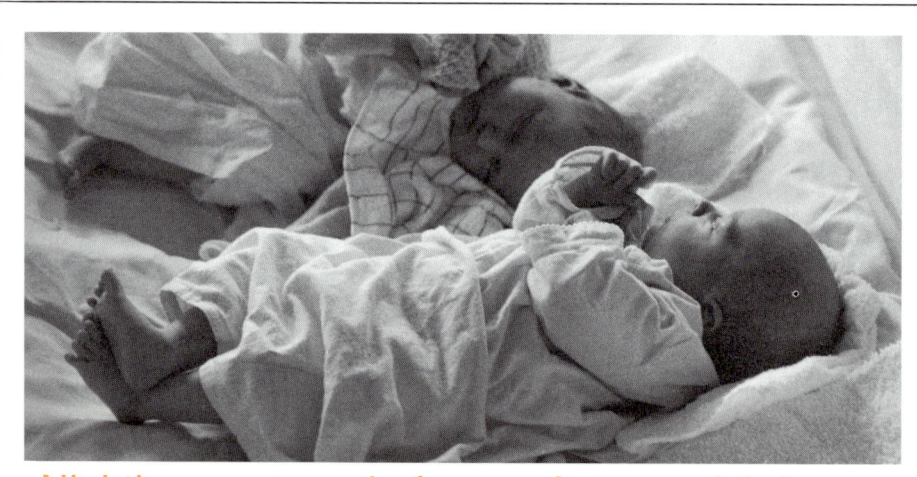
Nighties were made from soft, warm fabric.

1950s

Older baby girls wore dresses knitted from wool or made from pretty fabrics. Boys wore knitted jackets and leggings. Most baby clothes were in pale colours such as blue, pink, lemon or white.

Most mums could knit clothes like these.

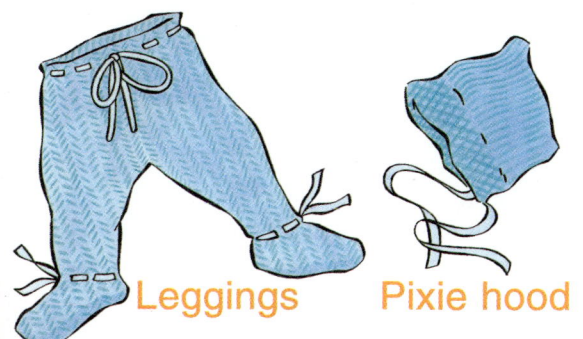

Leggings　　Pixie hood　　Bootees

Vest

When grandparents were toddlers

Boy toddlers wore short trousers. Girls wore dresses or skirts and jumpers.

Grandma

Grandad

Toddlers spent a lot of time in their prams.

1950s

The toddler is wearing a siren suit.

When children went outside they sometimes wore a **siren suit**. This was fastened by a long zip. Some clothes were bought from shops, some were made at home.

Great grandparents as babies

Babies were wrapped up tightly. It was not easy for them to move.

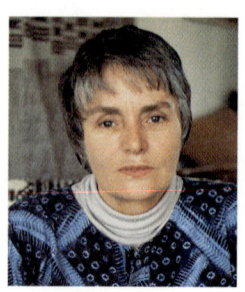

Great grandmother

Great grandfather

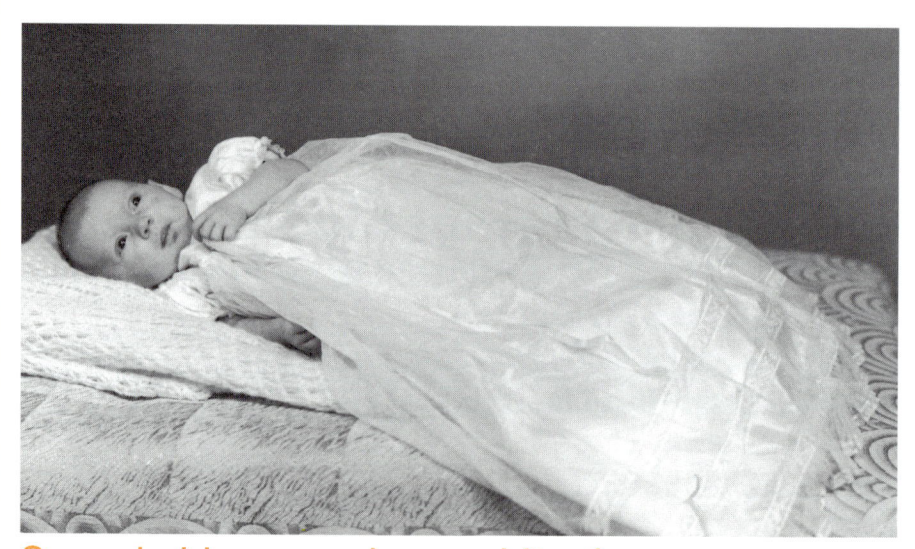

Some babies wore long, white, fancy gowns when they were christened.

1930s

It was difficult for babies to move in their tight clothes.

Mums used to wrap their babies tightly in a white blanket or shawl. They thought this would help their babies' bones to grow straight. When they were a bit older, boy babies were often dressed in pale blue and girls were dressed in pink. Most baby clothes were knitted.

Great grandparents as toddlers

Little girls wore dresses with **embroidered** patterns on the front.

Great grandmother

Great grandfather

Boys wore **rompers**. They could crawl and play in these clothes.

This romper suit was fastened with buttons.

1930s

Girl toddlers wore very short dresses and had knickers to match.

Rompers sometimes had a flap at the back which was unbuttoned when the toddler went on the potty. Toddlers wore ankle socks and soft shoes which had a strap round the ankle. Their shoes were fastened with buttons.

What babies wore long ago

Newborn babies were wrapped up in a piece of soft, white sheet.
Some babies wore woollen vests. Babies' nappies were made of **muslin**.

Boys wore long petticoats until they were potty trained.

1910s

Babies were carried to show off the long dresses.

In rich families, small babies wore long, white, fancy dresses and lacy shawls. They wore **bonnets** to keep their heads warm.

Girl and boy babies were dressed in similar clothes.

What toddlers wore long ago

The photographs below are very old.

Toddlers were dressed to look like little adults.

Toddlers even wore fancy clothes to play in.

Poor children wore clothes older children had grown out of.

1910s

Glossary

Bodysuit One piece of clothing that fits the whole body.

Bonnet A cloth or knitted hat with tapes that are tied under the chin.

Catsuit A bodysuit without sleeves.

Cotton A fabric that is cool to wear.

Crimplene A fabric that is easy to wash.

Denim A fabric that is hardwearing.

Embroidery Coloured threads sewn on to material to make a pattern.

Fabrics Materials made of cloth.

Flared Trousers with wide bottoms.

Maternal Related on your mum's side of the family.

Muslin A thin cotton fabric.

Nylon A thin fabric, which is easy to wash and dry, and does not need ironing.

Paternal Related on your dad's side of the family.

Rompers A play suit for boy toddlers.

Siren suit A suit which covered the whole body. It had a hood and was worn outdoors.

Terry towelling A material made of towel, which was used for babies' nappies.

Index

bodysuits 4, 5, 8
buttons 11, 18, 19
catsuits 8, 9
christening gowns 16
cotton 5, 11
crimplene 10
denim 10
dresses 7, 9, 10, 11, 13, 14, 18, 19, 21
family tree 2, 3
jackets 13
jumpers 7, 14
knitted clothes 13, 17
leggings, 7, 13
nappies 4, 8, 12, 20
nighties 12
nylon 10, 11
petticoats 20
rompers 18, 19
shawls 17, 21
shoes 11, 19
shirts 11
shorts 7
siren suits 15
skirts 7, 11, 14
socks 19
tee shirts 7
track suits 7
trousers 7, 11, 14
vests 4, 5, 20
wool, woollen 5, 13, 20
zips 15